Editorial Project Manager
Erica N. Russikoff, M.A.

Editor in Chief
Brent L. Fox, M. Ed.

Creative Director
Sarah M. Fournier

Cover Artist
Diem Pascarella

Illustrator
Crystal-Dawn Keitz

Imaging
Amanda R. Harter

Publisher
Mary D. Smith, M.S. Ed.

Teacher Created Resources
TCR 8311

5+

CHANGE YOUR MINDSET

Growth Mindset Activities for the Classroom

- Teaches, demonstrates, and reinforces a growth mindset

- Contains 12 comprehensive units, each one illustrating a different inspirational person and growth-mindset mantra

- Includes reading passages and individual, small-group, and whole-class practice that require short and long responses

Teacher Created Resources

Author
Samantha Chagollan

Teacher Created Resources
12621 Western Avenue
Garden Grove, CA 92841
www.teachercreated.com
ISBN: 978-1-4206-8311-0

©2020 Teacher Created Resources
Reprinted, 2021
Made in U.S.A.

Teacher Created Resources

TABLE OF CONTENTS

INTRODUCTION

In 1988, a group of researchers, including Stanford psychology professor Carol Dweck, studied students' responses to failure.

Some students rebounded well, while others were derailed by simple setbacks.

After extensive research with thousands of students, Dr. Dweck came up with the terms *fixed mindset* and *growth mindset* to encapsulate the differences between how all of us think about learning.

Simply put, having a growth mindset means you believe that you can and will improve with effort. A fixed mindset, by comparison, means that you believe you have a fixed amount of intelligence or talent that will never change.

We all have these two mindsets, but what Dr. Dweck has shown is that students are more likely to succeed once they take on a growth mindset and understand that they can get better at anything with time and effort.

In a fixed mindset, challenges are avoided, criticism is ignored, and students feel threatened by the success of others and are quick to give up when things get hard.

In a growth mindset, mistakes are seen as learning opportunities, challenges are welcomed, and students persevere with effort, leading to a desire to learn even more.

Teaching students about a growth mindset and the science behind it, including brain plasticity, has helped countless students to grasp the idea that they can achieve their dreams, no matter their starting points.

The activities in this book support the growth-mindset philosophy. With practice and positive reinforcement, students will be able to adopt this flexible, supportive, and uplifting perspective.

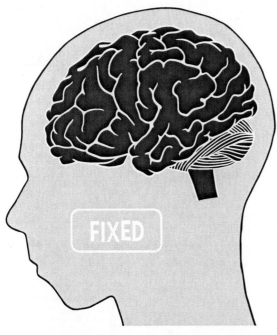

knowledge is unchanging

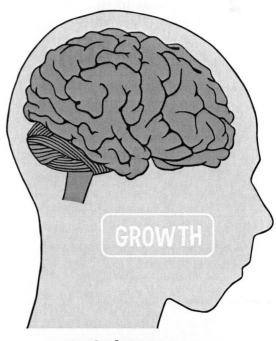

knowledge can grow

HOW TO USE THIS BOOK

For practical application in the classroom, this book provides 12 units that are each focused on one of the following growth-mindset mantras:

- ⭐ I will do my best.
- ⭐ I can put in more time and effort.
- ⭐ I can learn from my mistakes.
- ⭐ I believe I can do it.
- ⭐ I can reach my goals.
- ⭐ I am not afraid of difficult tasks.

- ⭐ I can come up with creative solutions.
- ⭐ I can improve with practice.
- ⭐ I value thoughtful feedback.
- ⭐ I am capable of learning new things.
- ⭐ I can keep going when things are tough.
- ⭐ I can train my brain.

Each unit includes an overview for the teacher and six student activities to support each mantra.

Reading Passage: To help students understand the meaning of the mantra, each unit includes a nonfiction narrative that features the story of someone who exemplifies that mantra.

Short-Answer Activity: After reading, students are asked a handful of questions that will check for understanding and provide potential talking points for a larger class discussion about the mantra.

Small-Group Activity: Students are asked to gather in small groups and collaborate to gain a deeper understanding.

Whole-Class Activity: The class is asked to reflect on their learning together; whole-class activities provide a perfect forum for learning about growth-mindset principles and practices, too.

Journal Prompt: Students are given the opportunity to reflect on what they have learned in the unit.

Growing Beyond: An extension activity is presented to take learning beyond the classroom for deeper understanding. *Note:* This activity is listed on the lesson plan and does not have its own page.

All the activities in this book have been aligned to the Common Core State Standards (CCSS). A correlations chart is included on pages 79–80.

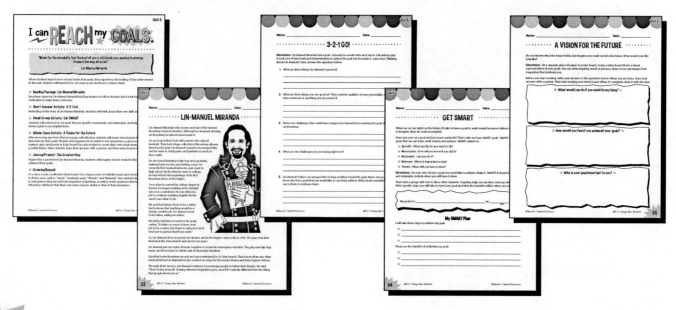

TEACHER SELF-ASSESSMENT

Before you dive into teaching growth mindset, it's a good idea to know where you stand.

Read each statement and note whether this is something you always, sometimes, or never do or say. On a separate piece of paper, take notes that might be helpful for your own self-reflection.

	Always	Sometimes	Never
1. I am inspired when others around me succeed.	☐	☐	☐
2. I believe that intelligence can improve.	☐	☐	☐
3. I learn from my mistakes.	☐	☐	☐
4. When things get challenging, I am likely to give up.	☐	☐	☐
5. If something doesn't work, I try a different strategy.	☐	☐	☐
6. I receive feedback and criticism well.	☐	☐	☐
7. There are some things I am just not good at.	☐	☐	☐
8. I set goals and monitor my progress.	☐	☐	☐
9. I have a set way of doing things that works for me.	☐	☐	☐
10. Some students just aren't good at certain things.	☐	☐	☐
11. I love to learn new things.	☐	☐	☐
12. I notice when I am thinking negative thoughts, and I am able to change those thoughts to more encouraging ones.	☐	☐	☐

We all fluctuate between both fixed and growth mindsets, but it's important to know for yourself which side you favor.

In this assessment, items 4, 7, 9, and 10 are fixed-mindset statements. The rest are growth-mindset statements.

Each mantra featured in this book is a growth-mindset statement that you can reinforce in your classroom. The more you use and model these mantras for your students, the greater their understanding of the growth mindset will be.

PARENT LETTER

As you're teaching your students about growth mindset, bring parents into the picture so this attitude can be practiced at home, too.

Consider creating a parent letter that explains what the growth mindset is, and how parents can support their child's learning. Here's an example:

Dear Parents,

Many of us grew up believing that either we were smart or we weren't. We were either good at something or we weren't.

But now, through scientific research, we know that simply isn't true. Our brains can grow and change, and when students are aware of this, they can get inspired to learn more.

I'm working with your child to help develop a "growth mindset." Someone with a growth mindset gives their best effort, learns from mistakes, and finds creative solutions to problems.

I would love for you to help support this growth mindset at home, too. Here are some ideas for how you can help:

⭐ Remind your child that mistakes are okay. We all make them! Each time we try and fail, our brains get stronger, and this is how we learn to persevere when things get tough.

⭐ Praise effort over achievement. It's the process that counts, so compliment your child for the work they put in, the creativity they displayed, or the determination they showed.

⭐ Ask questions like, "How were you challenged today? What mistakes did you make? What did you learn?"

⭐ Help your child practice growth-mindset self-talk. If you hear your child say something like, "I can't do this!" have them try saying, "I can't do this yet, but I'll keep trying."

The more you can talk about this and model it for your child, the more they will understand that intelligence can change and achievement is never out of reach when effort is given.

Thank you for your support!

I will DO MY BEST.

> "If you want to change attitudes, start with a change in behavior."
>
> Katharine Hepburn

Teaching students what it means and how it feels to give their best effort can change their approach to challenges and obstacles.

⭐ Reading Passage: Katharine Hepburn

The most decorated actress of our time, Katharine Hepburn was once called "box office poison," but she defied critics and made film history through her hard work.

⭐ Short-Answer Activity: Best of the Best

Students will reflect on the story of Katharine Hepburn and how she demanded the best from herself and from others.

⭐ Small-Group Activity: Common Ground

In small groups, students will discuss what it means and how it feels to do your best, then individually complete a graphic organizer to record similarities.

⭐ Whole-Class Activity: Best of Friends

In pairs, students will interview each other about their "best" qualities and skills, then introduce their partners to the class.

⭐ Journal Prompt: Be Your Best

With these journal prompts, students will have the opportunity to reflect on a proud moment and the motivation they need to push through challenges.

⭐ Growing Beyond

As a class, discuss the idea of winning an award for achievement, like the Academy Awards. Talk about the idea that sometimes, even when we give our best efforts, we don't take home an award. Discuss what it means to give your very best, no matter who is watching or if there is recognition at the end. Remind students that when they do their best, they can always be proud of what they achieve, whether or not there is an award to be won.

Ask students to write and sign an effort promise that can be posted in the classroom as a reminder: I promise to give my best effort and not quit until I'm proud.

Name: _____   Date: _____

KATHARINE HEPBURN

Katharine Hepburn was the first woman to win four Academy Awards.

And yet, at one time, she was considered a failure. She had a string of movies that flopped at the box office, and critics thought she could never bounce back.

But Katharine proved them all wrong. How? By staying true to herself and working hard to give her best in every performance.

Katharine was born in 1907. Her parents encouraged her to speak her mind and work hard at school and athletics.

She always loved performing, but she truly fell in love with acting in college. Katharine started acting in plays on and off Broadway in New York City. A talent scout saw her perform and gave her the chance to audition for her first movie in 1932. She got the part, and her career took off.

Katharine was different from other actors of her time. She never hesitated to voice her opinions, and she wore pants and other casual clothes when other actresses wore glamorous dresses.

She had high standards—for herself and for others. She only wanted to work with the best because she gave her best in every performance.

Katharine won her first Academy Award in 1933 for *Morning Glory*, her third film. Then came the flops. Audiences did not like most of the movies she was in from 1933–1938. Critics labeled her "box office poison," meaning that any movie she was in was bound to fail.

But Katharine made a comeback with her performance in *The Philadelphia Story* on Broadway. The play was a hit! Katharine bought the rights to the story for a movie, with the agreement that she would be the star. The 1940 film was a huge success with both audiences and critics.

Katharine Hepburn went on to win three more Academy Awards for Best Actress, and she became one of the most famous movie stars of all time.

Name: _____   **Date:** _____

BEST OF THE BEST

Directions: Answer these questions on your own, writing your answers below. Then pair up with another student and discuss your answers.

1. How do you think Katharine Hepburn felt when critics were calling her "box office poison"? Do you think it discouraged or encouraged her to work harder? Why do you think so?

   _____

   _____

   _____

2. What does it mean to give your best? What are some characteristics of a person who gives their best?

   _____

   _____

   _____

3. In the reading passage, we learn that Katharine bought the rights to *The Philadelphia Story* so that she could make it into a movie. Why do you think she did that? Do you think it was a good idea? Why or why not?

   _____

   _____

   _____

4. Katharine was dedicated to giving her best in every performance, and she wanted everyone around her to give their best, too. Do you think other people notice when you are not giving your best? Why or why not?

   _____

   _____

   _____

5. Complete this sentence and then explain your answer: I'm at my best when I…

   _____

   _____

   _____

Name: _____ **Date:** _____

· · · · · · · · · · · · · COMMON GROUND · · · · · · · · · · · · ·

Directions: Form a group with two to three other students. Discuss these questions together:

⭐ What does it feel like when you do your best?

⭐ How does it feel when you know you are not doing your best?

⭐ What might get in the way of you doing your best?

Listen to one another's answers and notice whether your answers have anything in common. Then add your ideas below; write words or phrases that reflect your own experience of doing your best, and those of your group members. Any words or phrases you have in common go in the middle.

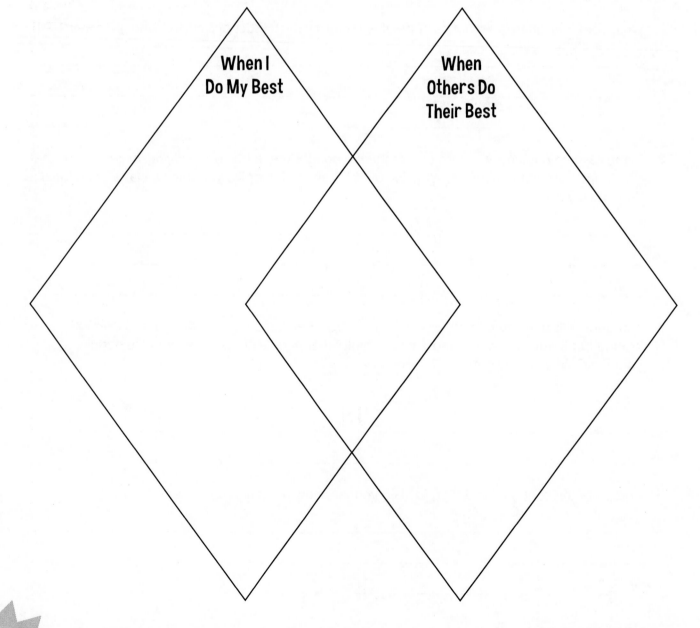

Name: _____ **Date:** _____

BEST OF FRIENDS

Just like Katharine Hepburn, we all have skills that we like to do and are good at. In this activity, you will pair up with another student and discover what they are best at.

Directions: Interview your partner and record their answers below. When it is your turn, introduce your partner to the class by sharing these answers.

⭐ **My partner's name:**

⭐ **Words others use to describe my partner:**

⭐ **What my partner loves to do:**

⭐ **What my partner is best at:**

⭐ **If my partner had a superpower, it would be...**

Name: _____   **Date:** _____

BE YOUR BEST

Winning four Academy Awards was a huge achievement for Katharine Hepburn. But sometimes, the things we are most proud of don't have awards that go with them. What is something you have worked hard at and are proud of? Who motivates you to do your best? How do you motivate yourself to do your best? Write your answers below.

_____

_____

_____

_____

_____

_____

_____

_____

_____

_____

_____

_____

_____

_____

_____

_____

_____

_____

_____

_____

I can PUT IN MORE TIME and EFFORT.

> "'I can't' are two words that have never been in my vocabulary.
> I believe in me more than anything in this world."
>
> **Wilma Rudolph**

Achieving goals takes time, effort, perseverance, and dedication. In this unit, students will discover that hard work pays off.

⭐ Reading Passage: Wilma Rudolph

Once a sickly child, Wilma Rudolph put in the time and effort to overcome her injuries and become the fastest woman in the world.

⭐ Short-Answer Activity: Determined to Succeed

Students will answer questions about Wilma Rudolph's story, reflecting on how her determination resulted in incredible success.

⭐ Small-Group Activity: Toss Up

Gather a bunch of small objects, such as mini marshmallows and erasers. Pair up students and give each student a cup. Ask them to stand three to four feet apart, increasing the distance as the game goes on. Students will need to work together and, with time and effort, achieve their collective goal.

⭐ Whole-Class Activity: Best Effort

In this timed writing exercise, students will choose one of four quotes about effort and write about how it aligns with their own beliefs. Tell students when to start and stop writing (suggested timing: seven to eight minutes of writing without stopping). When done, break up the class into groups by quote and ask them to discuss their answers.

⭐ Journal Prompt: Master Plan

It's been said that it takes 10,000 hours to become an expert at anything. In this journaling exercise, students will reflect on a skill they would like to master and think about a practical plan for achieving mastery.

⭐ Growing Beyond

As a class, watch the 1977 film *Wilma* about Wilma Rudolph's life. Discuss as a class the obstacles that Wilma had to overcome and the qualities of determination and confidence that helped lead her to success. Ask the class to reflect on what characteristics they might have in common with Wilma Rudolph.

Name: _____   **Date:** _____

WILMA RUDOLPH

As a child, Wilma Rudolph was told she would never walk again. No one would ever have guessed that she would become the "fastest woman in the world" when she grew up.

When Wilma was four years old, she was so sick with double pneumonia and scarlet fever that she almost died. Her illness left her with a paralyzed left leg, and she was forced to wear a brace just to move around.

Wilma's diagnosis was not good. But Wilma didn't give up the hope that she could improve. "My doctor told me I would never walk again. My mother told me I would. I believed my mother," said Wilma.

She was determined to get better. Her family helped by massaging her injured leg and driving her more than 90 miles for her physical therapy.

By the time she was six years old, Wilma was able to hop around on one leg. When she was eight, she could walk with a brace. At 11 years old, her mother found her playing basketball barefoot in the backyard.

Wilma never looked back. She worked hard to get on her high school basketball team and went to track camps during the summer.

The time and effort Wilma put into her training paid off. She made the 1956 Olympic track-and-field team, and won a bronze medal in Melbourne. Wilma also made the 1960 Olympic team. When she appeared at the Games in Rome, she broke three world records and won three gold medals.

Wilma was the first American woman to ever win three gold medals in track and field at an Olympic competition. Soon, she became known as the fastest woman in the world. Wilma was voted into the National Track and Field Hall of Fame and the US Olympic Hall of Fame.

Wilma Rudolph proved you could make your dreams come true with hard work and effort. She said, "Never underestimate the power of dreams and the influence of the human spirit. We are all the same in this notion. The potential for greatness lives within each of us."

Name: _____   **Date:** _____

········· # DETERMINED TO SUCCEED ·········

Directions: Answer these questions on your own, writing your answers below.

1. Wilma Rudolph had the help of her family as she worked hard to get better. How do you think her life might have turned out if she didn't have anyone to help her? How important is it to have support?

_____

_____

_____

2. How do you think Wilma felt when doctors told her she would never walk again? How do you think she felt when her mother insisted she would walk again?

_____

_____

_____

3. Do you think it was challenging for Wilma to become an athlete after being so sick as a child? What is one thing you think helped her to keep training?

_____

_____

_____

4. You could say that Wilma was *determined* to follow her dreams. What are some other adjectives you would use to describe Wilma?

_____

_____

_____

5. How do you think Wilma felt when she won three gold medals—more than any other American woman ever had? Explain why you think she felt that way.

_____

_____

_____

Name: _____   **Date:** _____

· · · · · · · · · · · · · **TOSS UP** · · · · · · · · · · · · ·

Pat Riley, a former basketball coach, said, "If you have a positive attitude and constantly strive to give your best effort, eventually you will overcome your immediate problems and find you are ready for greater challenges."

As Pat suggests, you will need a positive attitude and a determined spirit to do well in this game. This game is all about effort and partnership. Work with your partner to succeed, and then write about your experience below.

Directions: Grab your cup and stand across from your partner. If you have the cup full of objects, your job is to try to toss them underhand into your partner's cup. If you have the empty cup, your job is to try to catch the object your partner throws. Your goal is to get all of the objects from one cup to the other, without dropping any on the ground. To make it more interesting, every time you catch an object, you each take a step back.

You may have to go slowly, taking some time and effort to come up with a strategy that is effective. When you're done, come back to this page and answer the questions below. Good luck!

★ How did it feel when it was challenging? Did you want to give up?

_____

_____

_____

_____

★ What did you say to your partner to encourage them to keep going?

_____

_____

_____

_____

★ What does it feel like when your efforts pay off?

_____

_____

_____

Name: _____ **Date:** _____

BEST EFFORT

Directions: Read these quotes about effort and highlight the one you like best. Once your teacher tells you to start, write about how the quote you chose is similar to your own beliefs about effort. When your teacher tells you to stop writing, discuss your answers with a small group.

"Continuous effort—not strength or intelligence— is the key to unlocking our potential."

—Winston Churchill

"All things are difficult before they are easy."

—Thomas Fuller

"Just try to be the best you can be; never cease trying to be the best you can be. That's in your power."

—John Wooden

"We all have dreams. But in order to make dreams come into reality, it takes an awful lot of determination, dedication, self-discipline, and effort."

—Jesse Owens

_____

_____

_____

_____

_____

_____

_____

_____

_____

_____

_____

_____

_____

_____

_____

Name: _____ **Date:** _____

MASTER PLAN

Some people say it takes 10,000 hours of learning to become an expert at anything.

What is something that you would like to be an expert at? What is a skill you would like to master? Who might be able to help you master this skill? What is a plan you could make to work on becoming an expert?

_____

_____

_____

_____

_____

_____

_____

_____

_____

_____

_____

_____

_____

_____

_____

_____

_____

_____

_____

_____

_____

I can LEARN from my MISTAKES.

> "Expect me to give my all. That's what I do every time I have a show. Give my all."
>
> Bruno Mars

Everyone makes mistakes, but sometimes students get so focused on the error that they miss the valuable lesson that comes with it. In this unit, students will experiment with making mistakes and learn how to deal with them when they happen.

★ Reading Passage: Bruno Mars

The hitmaker's first record deal fell apart just months after he signed it, but Bruno Mars didn't let that mistake stop him from becoming an international superstar.

★ Short-Answer Activity: Making Mistakes

Reflecting on the story of Bruno Mars, students will write about what can be learned from making mistakes and then share their answers in small groups.

★ Small-Group Activity: Art in the Dark

Sometimes, students are afraid to make mistakes. So, to practice not being in control of everything, students will make something beautiful out of a mistake. Turn out the lights for the first two to three minutes of this activity and ask students to start creating their art. When you turn the lights back on, ask them to notice what they created and how it might be different from what they were envisioning. Can they find the beauty in it? Then have them finish their art with the lights on.

★ Whole-Class Activity: The Book of Mistakes

As a class, read *The Book of Mistakes* by Corinna Luyken. Afterward, some short-answer questions and a class discussion will help crystallize the lessons learned.

★ Journal Prompt: Mistakes or Lessons?

What can you learn from your mistakes? Students will reflect on what they have learned about the beautiful lessons that can be gained from making mistakes.

★ Growing Beyond

Challenge your students to create more art from "mistakes." Prepare some blank pieces of paper ahead of time, with interesting rips or folds, blots of ink or paint, or other alterations that may look like mistakes. Break the class up into small groups and distribute the "mistakes," asking them to turn them into their own pieces of art. Ask them to encourage one another as they create. Display their finished art in the classroom as a reminder that mistakes can turn into something beautiful.

Name: _____ Date: _____

BRUNO MARS

Grammy-winning artist Bruno Mars was just 18 years old when he signed his first record deal with Motown Records. He was destined for success, but it didn't come without a few mistakes along the way.

Bruno Mars was born in Hawaii to a musical family. From four years old, Bruno was performing on stage with his family. He learned how to play the guitar, piano, and drums without taking a single lesson. Music and entertainment were just always around him.

It was no surprise then that Bruno wanted to move to Los Angeles to follow his musical dreams as soon as he was done with high school. Right away, he was offered a deal with Motown Records, and he didn't hesitate to sign it.

But the deal fizzled out, and by the time Bruno was 19, Motown had dropped him. Surely, a part of him must have felt as though moving to LA and trying to be an artist had all been a mistake. This could have devastated Bruno, but instead, he let it fuel his desire to work harder.

"I didn't want to give up. My goal was, 'I'm not going to go back home. I'm not going back to Hawaii and face my friends and family saying it didn't pan out. I've got to do something.' I think I grew. I grew as an artist. I grew as a writer. I wrote songs every day. I started producing. And you know, practice is what you need."

Bruno started writing and producing songs for other artists, which helped him make a name for himself. Within a few years, he was offered a new record deal at Atlantic Records.

Soon after came a string of number-one hits, awards, and sold-out tours. Bruno is one of the best-selling artists of all time, and he has won more than 10 Grammy Awards, including Album of the Year and Song of the Year. He also performed in the half-time show of the Superbowl.

But none of that would have happened if his first record deal with Motown hadn't flopped. Today, Bruno says he is sort of grateful that deal never worked out. "It was my fault. I wasn't ready yet. And because the thing with Motown didn't work, that's how I became a producer, that's why I have a story."

Name: _____ Date: _____

MAKING MISTAKES

Directions: Thinking about Bruno's story, answer the questions below. Then form a group with two to three other students and discuss your answers.

1. Do you think Bruno signing his first deal with Motown Records was a mistake? Why or why not?

_____

_____

_____

2. Bruno said that he didn't want to go home and face his family and friends after being dropped by Motown. If you were Bruno's friend at that time, what is one thing you would have said to him about the deal falling apart?

_____

_____

_____

3. What lesson do you think Bruno learned from his mistakes?

_____

_____

_____

4. Do you think you can learn from the mistakes you make? Why or why not?

_____

_____

_____

5. After his deal fell through, Bruno said he wouldn't give up. Do you think he had a good attitude? Why or why not?

_____

_____

_____

#8311 Change Your Mindset

Name: _____   **Date:** _____

ART IN THE DARK

Have you ever been so afraid of messing up that you didn't even want to do something? It's important to remember that everyone makes mistakes. To get used to how it feels to make a mistake, you are going to practice messing up.

Directions: While waiting for instructions, think about these questions: What does a perfect day look like for you? What are you doing? What are you wearing? Who is with you?

When you're told it's time to begin, draw your perfect day below.

Name: _____   **Date:** _____

· · · · · · · · · · THE BOOK OF MISTAKES · · · · · · · · ·

In *The Book of Mistakes*, the artist makes many mistakes. But the artist also ends up creating something beautiful out of those mistakes.

Making a mistake once doesn't mean we will never make one again. In fact, making mistakes is how we learn valuable lessons. Mistakes teach us to go more slowly, try again, and attempt a different strategy next time.

How do you react when you make a mistake? Do you learn from it and try to turn it into something beautiful?

Directions: Write your answers to the questions below. Then share your answers in a class discussion.

1. What do you say to yourself when you make a mistake?

   _____

   _____

   _____

2. What do you say to other people when they mess up?

   _____

   _____

   _____

3. When you make a mistake, do you try again or do you give up? Give an example.

   _____

   _____

   _____

   _____

4. What is one thing you would like to improve but are afraid you will mess up?

   _____

   _____

   _____

   _____

Name: _____ **Date:** _____

· · · · · · · · · MISTAKES OR LESSONS? · · · · · · · · ·

Albert Einstein said, "A person who never made a mistake never tried anything new."

Thinking about what you learned, both from Bruno Mars's story and *The Book of Mistakes*, what do you now know about making mistakes that you didn't know before?

What is one mistake you have made that taught you a valuable lesson?

_____

_____

_____

_____

_____

_____

_____

_____

_____

_____

_____

_____

_____

_____

_____

_____

_____

_____

_____

_____

I BELIEVE I can DO IT.

> "Break through that, all the judgement. Never let anything hold you back."
>
> ~ Jessica Cox

In order to soar, we must believe in ourselves. Self-confidence gives students the resilience to keep learning, despite any obstacles that may appear. In this unit, students learn how self-belief can propel learning and growth.

★ Reading Passage: Jessica Cox

The first pilot without arms, Jessica Cox is an incredible inspiration whose self-confidence helped her achieve her dreams.

★ Short-Answer Activity: Learning to Fly

After reading Jessica's story, students will reflect on her belief in herself and examine what they can take away from her example.

★ Small-Group Activity: Three Nice Things

In small groups, students will say three nice things about one another, and then themselves, building self-confidence and positive collaboration.

★ Whole-Class Activity: I Am, We Are

Students will create art that completes the statement "I am…" If possible, have magazines available from which students can cut out images to include in their art. Then, as a class, discover what qualities students have in common. Create a poster with common attributes.

★ Journal Prompt: Fearlessly Brave

To overcome fear, we must believe in ourselves. In this writing exercise, students will journal about one fear they have that they would like to overcome.

★ Growing Beyond

Ask students to interview an expert; this could be a family member, a friend, or an adult relative who the student feels is an expert at self-confidence. The student should record answers to these questions:

- ★ What does it mean to believe in yourself?
- ★ What is one thing you have achieved that you didn't think you could do at first?
- ★ What did you say to yourself in order to achieve it?
- ★ What advice would you give me about believing in yourself?

Once interviews are complete, ask students to share their findings with the class and discuss some of the common threads in the responses.

Name: _____ Date: _____

JESSICA COX

Jessica Cox was born without arms, but she has learned how to fly. She is the first armless person to earn a pilot's license and fly solo.

How does someone without arms decide they are going to learn how to fly?

Jessica says it helps that when she was growing up, her parents encouraged her to do everything that other kids with arms could do. She learned to do every task with her feet—from drinking out of a glass and eating with a fork to coloring and playing.

For a while, she tried prosthetic arms. But they just never felt natural to her. After wearing them for 11 years, she decided to take them off. Jessica never looked back.

"I do not have arms, but that is not what determines what I can do," Jessica said.

Her belief in herself never wavered. She went to college and earned a degree in psychology and communication. She had already accomplished so much, but there was one fear left she wanted to overcome. Jessica had always had a fear of flying.

She believed she could get over this fear, and she wanted to try. For three years, she took flight lessons and learned how to fly a plane with her feet. Finally, she was a certified pilot. Jessica became the first person in aviation history to fly by using her feet.

And that is not all Jessica Cox can do. She trained in tae kwon do for many years and earned a black belt. In training, she also met her husband, Patrick. Jessica has also learned how to surf, scuba-dive, and play the piano.

For Jessica, it's not about whether she can do something—it's about how she can do it. She said, "I had to—out of necessity—develop that. Because that was how I had to approach everything. I was looking at it as: how can I do this with my feet instead?"

Today, Jessica is a motivational speaker who encourages people to overcome challenges and follow their dreams. She has unique experience that shows others that if you believe you can do it, there is really nothing to stop you from achieving the impossible.

Name: _____ Date: _____

LEARNING TO FLY

Directions: Thinking about Jessica's story, answer the questions below. Then find a partner and discuss your answers.

1. Jessica had the confidence to believe in herself, which allowed her to learn how to do everything with her feet instead of her hands. What are some adjectives you would use to describe Jessica?

   _____

   _____

   _____

2. How are you similar to or different from Jessica? Explain your answer.

   _____

   _____

   _____

3. Jessica's family was very supportive and encouraging. Who do you have in your life that helps you believe in yourself? How do they help you?

   _____

   _____

   _____

4. Sometimes, when we try to do something new, it can feel uncomfortable or scary. When you are learning a new skill, what do you say to yourself? Does that help you, or does it make it harder?

   _____

   _____

   _____

5. When Jessica earned her pilot's license, her dream came true. What is one thing you have achieved that you are proud of? How did you feel when it happened?

   _____

   _____

   _____

Name: _____   Date: _____

THREE NICE THINGS

Jessica Cox had a strong belief in herself—that she could do anything she put her mind to, despite her obstacles.

Even the most confident person sometimes doesn't see the good that others see. In this exercise, you will get a chance to hear some nice things that your classmates think about you.

Directions: Find two other students and form a group of three. Sit in a circle, facing one another. Take turns saying three nice things about one another. Each thing you say must be positive and true. Write what your partners say about you below. Then, at the bottom, say and write three nice things to yourself.

★ **Three Nice Things from** _____ **to Me** ★

1. _____
2. _____
3. _____

★ **Three Nice Things from** _____ **to Me** ★

1. _____
2. _____
3. _____

★ **Three Nice Things from Me to Me** ★

1. _____
2. _____
3. _____

Name: _____   **Date:** _____

· · · · · · · · · · · · I AM, WE ARE · · · · · · · · · · · ·

Directions: Who are you? What are the qualities that define you? Complete the sentence "I am…" with art. Draw, write, make a collage—it's up to you. You could include skills you've mastered, qualities of your personality, or beliefs you have about yourself. Get creative!

When you're done, discuss as a class and find what qualities you have in common with your classmates. Create a "We are…" poster together for your classroom that includes everything you have in common.

I am...

Name: _____   **Date:** _____

FEARLESSLY BRAVE

Jessica Cox said, "If you would've asked me about getting a pilot's license before 2005, I'd say you were crazy. After I graduated college, a fighter pilot asked me if I wanted to go up on a flight in a single-engine plane. I always had a fear about being in an airplane, but I took this opportunity to go up on my first flight in a single-engine rather than a big commercial plane I was accustomed to. I was hooked and made a commitment to become a pilot. I wanted to motivate others to not let fear stand in the way of their opportunities."

To achieve her dreams, Jessica had to overcome some of her fears, including the fear of flying. What is one thing you are afraid of that you would like to overcome? What are some small steps you could take toward overcoming your fear? Who could help you with this?

_____

_____

_____

_____

_____

_____

_____

_____

_____

_____

_____

_____

_____

_____

_____

_____

_____

_____

I can REACH my GOALS.

> "Allow for the possibility that the best of you is still inside you, waiting to emerge. Prepare the way, bit by bit."
>
> Lin-Manuel Miranda

When students learn how to set and attain their goals, they experience the feeling of true achievement. In this unit, students will learn how to set smart goals and how to achieve them.

★ Reading Passage: Lin-Manuel Miranda

Broadway superstar Lin-Manuel Miranda had big dreams of a life in theater, but it took hard work and dedication to make them come true.

★ Short-Answer Activity: 3-2-1 Go!

Reflecting on the story of Lin-Manuel Miranda, students will think about their own skills and challenges.

★ Small-Group Activity: Get SMART

Students will learn how to set goals that are specific, measurable, and achievable, and help one another devise a plan to accomplish them.

★ Whole-Class Activity: A Vision for the Future

After answering questions that encourage self-reflection, students will create vision boards for themselves that embody their goals. Provide old magazines from which to cut out pictures, patterned papers, markers, glue, and poster or foam board for each student to create their own visual reminder of their possible future. Have students share their answers with a partner and their vision boards with the class.

★ Journal Prompt: The Greatest Day

Inspired by a quote from Lin-Manuel Miranda, students will imagine what it would be like if they achieved their goals.

★ Growing Beyond

As a class, create a collective vision board. Use a large poster or bulletin board, and consider sectioning it off into areas, such as "career," "academic goals," "friends," and "financial." Give students the opportunity to add drawings or pictures they cut out from magazines, as well as words or phrases that have meaning. What they will find is that their own vision may be similar to that of their classmates.

Name: _____   Date: _____

LIN-MANUEL MIRANDA

Lin-Manuel Miranda is the creator and star of the famous Broadway musical *Hamilton*. Although he dreamed of being on Broadway, he almost never made it.

He grew up in New York with parents who adored musicals. They had a huge collection of Broadway albums they loved to play. Lin-Manuel's parents encouraged him and his sister to study piano and perform as much as they could.

He also loved listening to hip-hop and rap music, making home movies, and writing songs. He wrote his first musical before he even went to high school. By the time he went to college, he had written the beginnings of his first Broadway show, *In the Heights*.

Soon after he earned his college degree in theater, he began teaching at his old high school as a substitute. He was offered a job to continue teaching English. But he wasn't sure what to do.

His goal had always been to be a writer, but he knew that teaching would be a steady, sensible job. Lin-Manuel wrote to his father, asking for advice.

His father told him to reach for his goals, saying, "It makes no sense to leave your job to be a writer, but I have to tell you to do it. You have to pursue that if you want."

So, Lin-Manuel chose to pursue his dreams, and *In the Heights* came to life in 2008. The play won Best Musical at the Tony Awards and ran for two years.

Lin-Manuel put two styles of music together to create his masterpiece *Hamilton*. The play uses hip-hop music and show tunes to tell the tale of Alexander Hamilton.

Hamilton broke Broadway records and was nominated for 16 Tony Awards. That is more than any other musical before! Lin-Manuel has also worked on songs for the movies *Moana* and *Mary Poppins Returns*.

Through all his success, Lin-Manuel continues to encourage people to follow their dreams. He said, "That's being yourself. Chasing wherever inspiration goes, even if it's radically different from the thing that people know you as."

Name: _____ **Date:** _____

3-2-1 GO!

Directions: Lin-Manuel Miranda had a goal: someday he would write and star in a Broadway play. It took a lot of hard work and determination to achieve his goal, but he made it come true. Thinking about Lin-Manuel's story, answer the questions below.

1. What are three things Lin-Manuel is good at?

   _____

   _____

   _____

2. What are three things you are good at? They could be qualities of your personality, skills you have mastered, or anything you are proud of.

   _____

   _____

   _____

3. Name two challenges that could have stopped Lin-Manuel from reaching his goal of being on Broadway.

   _____

   _____

   _____

4. What are two challenges you are facing right now?

   _____

   _____

   _____

5. Lin-Manuel's father encouraged him to keep working toward his goal. Name one person you know who has a goal that you would like to see them achieve. Write down something you will say to them to motivate them.

   _____

   _____

   _____

Name: _____   Date: _____

GET SMART

When we set our sights on the future, it helps to have a goal to work toward because it allows our minds to imagine what we could accomplish.

Have you ever set a goal and just never reached it? That's why we have SMART goals. SMART goals are goals that we can track, work toward, and achieve. SMART stands for…

⭐ **S**pecific: What exactly do you want to do?

⭐ **M**easurable: How will you know if you did it?

⭐ **A**ttainable: Can you do it?

⭐ **R**elevant: Why is it important to you?

⭐ **T**imely: When will you have it done?

Directions: On your own, choose a goal you would like to achieve. Make it SMART! It should be specific and attainable. Include when you will have it done.

Then form a group with two to three other students. Together, help one another come up with a plan. Write specific steps you will take to meet your goal and what the benefits will be when you achieve it.

My goal is to _____ by _____.
(date)

My SMART Plan

I will take these steps to achieve my goal:

⭐ _____

⭐ _____

⭐ _____

These are the benefits of achieving my goal:

⭐ _____

⭐ _____

⭐ _____

Name: _____ **Date:** _____

A VISION FOR THE FUTURE

No one knows what the future holds, but imagine you could see into the future. What would your life look like?

Directions: On a separate piece of paper or poster board, create a vision board that is a visual representation of your goals. You can write inspiring words or phrases, draw, or cut out images from magazines that motivate you.

Before you start creating, write your answers to the questions below. When you are done, share your answers with a partner. Then start creating your vision board. When it's complete, share it with the class.

★ **What would you do if you could do anything?** ★

★ **How would you feel if you achieved your goals?** ★

★ **Why is your goal important to you?** ★

Name: _____   **Date:** _____

· · · · · · · · · · · THE GREATEST DAY · · · · · · · · · · ·

Lin-Manuel Miranda said, "Every day has the potential to be the greatest day of your life."

Imagine that you've achieved the goals you have set for yourself, and it's the greatest day of your life. What would the greatest day of your life look like? Who would be there with you? What would you be doing? How would you feel?

_____

_____

_____

_____

_____

_____

_____

_____

_____

_____

_____

_____

_____

_____

_____

_____

_____

_____

_____

_____

I am NOT afraid of DIFFICULT TASKS.

> "Students must have initiative; they should not be mere imitators.
> They must learn to think and act for themselves—and be free."
>
> Cesar Chavez

It takes courage to face difficult tasks. In this unit, students will discover how to dig deep and find the initiative and bravery to move toward difficulties, instead of away from them.

★ Reading Passage: Cesar Chavez

For more than 30 years, Cesar Chavez overcame difficulties to fight for the rights of migrant farmworkers. He is an example of courage in the face of hardship.

★ Short-Answer Activity: Staying Strong

After learning about Cesar Chavez, students will reflect on the qualities of this leader who faced difficulty with courage. Once students have talked through questions with partners, they will answer the questions on their own.

★ Small-Group Activity: Acts of Courage

What does it mean to be courageous? Students will recount a story of courage they have heard or witnessed and share it in a small group.

★ Whole-Class Activity: Have Some Courage

To inspire and encourage one another, students will record motivational phrases on sticky notes that can be displayed on a bulletin board in the classroom. The idea is to "take what you need"—so when things get hard, students can borrow a sticky note from the wall of courage to place on their desks as a reminder to persevere.

★ Journal Prompt: Face the Fear

Students will consider one fear that might be holding them back and journal about gathering courage to face any challenges that may lie ahead.

★ Growing Beyond

As a class, discover more about Cesar Chavez. Read *Harvesting Hope: The Story of Cesar Chavez* by Kathleen Krull, watch a short online biographical video, or watch the feature film *Cesar Chavez*. Conduct a class discussion around these questions:

- ★ How did Cesar take initiative to try to solve the inequalities he observed?

- ★ What are the qualities of leadership?

- ★ How can you take responsibility for your own learning experience?

Name: _____   **Date:** _____

CESAR CHAVEZ

Cesar Chavez fought for the rights of farm and migrant workers all of his life. It was never easy, but he never gave up.

Cesar learned about injustice very early in life. When Cesar was a child growing up in Yuma, Arizona, his family had their home and land taken from them illegally. They were forced to move to a *barrio*, a poor part of town.

Everyone in Cesar's family had to work. They became migrant farmworkers, working the fields up and down the coast of California. After eighth grade, Cesar went to work full-time, too, to help support his family.

Workers were made to perform tasks in unsafe conditions and around pesticides and other dangerous chemicals. They worked long hours, and they were not paid very much for their work. When they needed help, they had a hard time getting it.

After serving in the Navy, Cesar returned home and began learning more about workers' rights. He had seen how unfairly the workers were treated, and he was determined to make it better for them.

In 1962, Cesar founded the National Farm Workers Association, which later became the United Farm Workers. He knew that if the workers formed a union, their voices would be stronger together. As he said, "Together, all things are possible."

To help workers get the rights they deserved, he wanted to use only nonviolent protests. This meant using strikes and boycotts to try to be heard.

A *boycott* is when people stop buying something to protest. In 1984, Cesar led a boycott against grapes, asking everyone not to buy any more grapes until farmworkers were heard.

People from all over the country heard about the grape boycott and wanted to help. Cesar also fasted, meaning he stopped eating for several weeks and only drank water. He did this to bring attention to his cause.

During his lifetime, Cesar Chavez was devoted to helping the voices of poor workers be heard. It was a difficult task, but he kept going. He inspired a movement that helped increase wages and improve conditions for workers all over the country.

Name: _____ **Date:** _____

· · · · · · · · · · · · STAYING STRONG · · · · · · · · · · · ·

Directions: Thinking back on what you read about Cesar Chavez, pair up with another student and talk through the questions below. Then, individually, write your answers on the lines.

1. There were many difficulties that Cesar Chavez faced in his life. What are two you learned about in reading his story?

   _____

   _____

   _____

2. Why do you think Cesar wanted to bring farmworkers together? Do you think he was right?

   _____

   _____

   _____

3. What are three words you would use to describe Cesar Chavez? Explain why you chose each word.

   _____

   _____

   _____

4. Cesar kept fighting for justice, even when it became extremely difficult. What do you think it was that kept him fighting?

   _____

   _____

   _____

5. What do you think would have happened if Cesar had given up when things got hard?

   _____

   _____

   _____

Name: _____   Date: _____

· · · · · · · · · · · · · ACTS OF COURAGE · · · · · · · · · · · ·

As you read, think about how Cesar Chavez had to face many difficulties to reach his goals. Facing difficult tasks takes courage. *Courage* is the ability to do something that frightens you.

Directions: Form a group with two to three other students. On your own, write your answers to the first two questions below. Then share them with your group and answer the third question.

⭐ What is the most courageous act you have ever heard of or witnessed?

_____

_____

_____

_____

_____

_____

⭐ What is one thing you took away from that act of courage?

_____

_____

_____

_____

_____

_____

⭐ What did you learn by listening to the stories from the rest of your group?

_____

_____

_____

_____

_____

_____

Name: _____   Date: _____

HAVE SOME COURAGE

Directions: When things are difficult, you may need some courage to face them. As a class, create a bulletin board full of courage so that when you need some, you can be inspired. Use the space below to record some encouraging phrases that you or your classmates might need to hear if they are feeling afraid or worried. Then choose two or three favorites and write them on sticky notes to attach to the bulletin board. Here are some examples to get you started:

- ⭐ Nothing is impossible!
- ⭐ Never give up!
- ⭐ You've got this!

- ⭐ You have the power!
- ⭐ Just believe in yourself!
- ⭐ Your dreams are bigger than your fears!

Courage for My Class

Name: _____   **Date:** _____

· · · · · · · · · · · · FACE THE FEAR · · · · · · · · · · · · ·

We all face difficulties in life. And it's natural to be afraid of them or to want to avoid them. But as Cesar Chavez showed us, we can face difficulties with courage. Thinking about Cesar and his life, write answers to the questions below.

1. What is one thing you are afraid of that you would like to face?

   _____

   _____

   _____

   _____

   _____

   _____

2. Think of a moment when you felt courageous. What did it feel like? What did you do?

   _____

   _____

   _____

   _____

   _____

   _____

3. What will you do the next time you are confronted with a difficult task?

   _____

   _____

   _____

   _____

   _____

   _____

I can COME ★ UP with CREATIVE SOLUTIONS.

> "One child, one teacher, one book, one pen can change the world."
>
> Malala Yousafzai

Creativity is key—especially when students face obstacles they are not sure how to navigate. By exploring and expanding their creative skills, students are less likely to get frustrated and give up when difficulties arise.

★ Reading Passage: Malala Yousafzai

The youngest Nobel Prize winner is an advocate and activist who is finding creative solutions for a global issue.

★ Short-Answer Activity: Find Another Path

After reading Malala's story, students will think about ways in which she took action and found creative solutions to the problems she faced. Then students will share their answers with partners.

★ Small-Group Activity: 30 Ways

In small groups, students will generate creative ideas together. Choose an inanimate object that is easily found, such as an aluminum can, a pickle jar, or a stack of old newspapers. Break the class up into small groups and ask them to come up with 30 new ways to use the object. Give them 7–10 minutes to complete the task, and then ask a representative from each group to present their top five ideas to the class.

★ Whole-Class Activity: App-tastic Solutions

First, students will work together in small groups to design a smartphone app that solves a problem. Then each group will present their app to the class. Follow the presentations with a class discussion about collaboration and creativity.

★ Journal Prompt: Overcoming Hurdles

When times are tough, how do we react? Knowing what they have learned about coming up with creative solutions, students will explain how they will face future challenges.

★ Growing Beyond

Ask students to create the backstory behind a creative solution by having them write a news story. You provide the headline—it can be anything that gives a snapshot of a problem being solved, whether it's local or global. For example, "Student Finds Cure for the Common Cold," or "School Recycles Record Amount of Plastic." Ask students to explain how the problem was solved, and have them provide an illustration, too.

Name: _____   Date: _____

MALALA YOUSAFZAI

As a young girl, Malala Yousafzai already knew what she believed in. Malala wanted every girl to have an education.

When she was 11 years old, girls were suddenly forbidden to go to school where she lived. Her father was a teacher, and Malala had always loved school. She couldn't believe that she and her classmates were no longer allowed to have an education.

By the time she was 15, Malala had spoken out about girls' rights to learn. That made her a target, and she was shot on her way home from school.

Even after a long recovery, Malala knew she wanted to keep fighting. "It was then I knew I had a choice: I could live a quiet life or I could make the most of this new life I had been given. I determined to continue my fight until every girl could go to school."

Malala was 16 when she was asked to speak at the United Nations. She asked countries at the United Nations to commit to making sure every girl receives 12 years of education by 2030. They agreed to make educating girls a priority.

But many countries have not followed through on their promise. The biggest countries in Asia, Latin America, and Africa have not increased their budgets for education yet.

It might have been easy for Malala to give up on her goal, but she refused to believe she couldn't make her dreams come true. She knew she had to come up with a creative solution.

With her father's help, she started the Malala Fund, a charity that helps provide funds for girls' education. The fund invests in educators in communities where it is hard for girls to go to school.

In 2012, Malala's hard work was recognized when she won the Nobel Peace Prize. She is the youngest person to ever have been nominated—and to win.

Today, Malala continues to fight for girls all over the world, finding creative ways to solve the issue she is so passionate about.

Name: _____ **Date:** _____

FIND ANOTHER PATH

Directions: Now that you have read Malala's story, answer the questions below. Then share your answers with a partner.

1. Why do you think Malala is so passionate about educating girls? Why do you think it's important?

   _____

   _____

   _____

2. After she was shot, Malala faced a long and painful recovery. But she never gave up on her dream. How do you think Malala was able to keep fighting for what she believed in?

   _____

   _____

   _____

3. When Malala spoke at the United Nations, what did she ask them to do? Why do you think some countries have not followed through on their promise?

   _____

   _____

   _____

4. Instead of giving up when change wasn't happening, Malala founded the Malala Fund to help her cause. What would you have done in her position? What creative solutions can you come up with?

   _____

   _____

   _____

5. Malala said, "When the whole world is silent, even one voice becomes powerful." What is one cause that you care about? How do you fight for what you believe in?

   _____

   _____

   _____

Name: _____   Date: _____

· · · · · · · · · · · · 30 WAYS · · · · · · · · · · · ·

Directions: Form a group with two to three other students. Your teacher will show you an object, and you will be tasked with coming up with 30 new ways to use it.

As a group, work together to help generate creative ideas. Think of uses that could help solve a problem—any problem! Build on one another's ideas to come up with as many creative solutions as you can. Write them here. Then choose one representative to present your top five ideas to the class.

1 _____   16 _____

2 _____   17 _____

3 _____   18 _____

4 _____   19 _____

5 _____   20 _____

6 _____   21 _____

7 _____   22 _____

8 _____   23 _____

9 _____   24 _____

10 _____   25 _____

11 _____   26 _____

12 _____   27 _____

13 _____   28 _____

14 _____   29 _____

15 _____   30 _____

Name: _____   Date: _____

APP-TASTIC SOLUTIONS

Directions: Form a group with three to four other students. You will be imagining a problem-solving app! First, think about a problem that needs to be solved. It could be something in your neighborhood, your state, or the whole world. Write it below. Then answer the questions. Share your ideas with the class.

The problem I want to solve is: _____

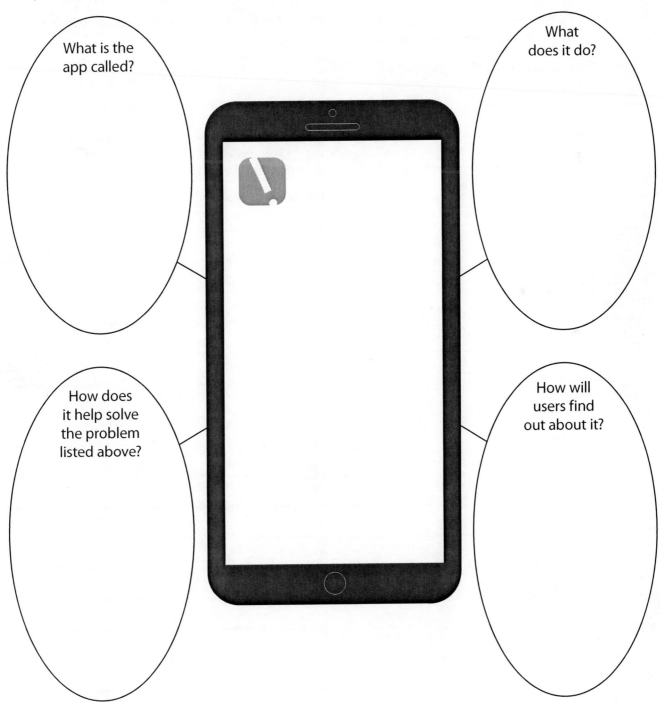

What is the app called?

What does it do?

How does it help solve the problem listed above?

How will users find out about it?

Name: _____ **Date:** _____

OVERCOMING HURDLES

You may not have faced the same kind of obstacles that Malala has faced, but everyone faces difficulties at some point.

Malala said, "To me, the moral of the story was that there will always be hurdles in life, but if you want to achieve a goal, you must continue."

How do you usually react when things get hard? Do you get frustrated and give up, or do you try to figure out a creative way to solve the problem?

The next time you face a challenge, what will you do?

_____

_____

_____

_____

_____

_____

_____

_____

_____

_____

_____

_____

_____

_____

_____

_____

_____

_____

I can IMPROVE with PRACTICE.

> **"A brave heart is a powerful weapon."**
>
> Rudy Garcia-Tolson

We often hear that "practice makes perfect"—but in reality, practice makes progress. In this unit, students will learn how hard work and dedication can make any dream achievable.

★ Reading Passage: Rudy Garcia-Tolson

Paralympic athlete Rudy Garcia-Tolson is a world-record breaker and gold medalist who never met a challenge he didn't like. Students will be inspired by his story of courage and hard work.

★ Short-Answer Activity: Practice Makes Progress

With Rudy's story in mind, students will reflect on the idea of practicing to make progress toward their goals. Then they will share their answers with partners.

★ Small-Group Activity: Walk a Mile

Have students watch the short YouTube video *A Day in the Life: Rudy Garcia-Tolson*. Then break the class up into small groups to complete the activity, in which students will imagine how Rudy would respond to one of three hypothetical situations. When complete, ask the groups to share their responses with the class.

★ Whole-Class Activity: A Real Juggling Act

Skills take practice, and in this exercise, students will have the chance to practice a physical skill and chart their improvement. Gather enough tennis or stress balls so that there is one for every four to five students. Allow students to practice in small groups to inspire class encouragement. Coach students by starting a timer and keeping it running for each side, so that students can record their progress.

★ Journal Prompt: Change the World

Inspired by Rudy's journey, students will reflect on a skill they would like to practice and a dream they would love to achieve.

★ Growing Beyond

Define a class goal that can be measured. It could be a skill to be mastered, a charitable donation the whole class will contribute to, or an achievement, such as books read over a period of time. Chart the progress visually so it is a constant reminder for the class. Consider offering a class reward for the progress made, as well as the final achievement.

Name: _____   Date: _____

RUDY GARCIA-TOLSON

Rudy Garcia-Tolson was born a little different—but he would grow up to change the world.

Because he was born with several rare birth defects, Rudy faced challenges from the beginning. By the time he was just five years old, he had already had more than 15 surgeries on his legs to try to straighten them out.

Knowing that he did not want to spend his life in a wheelchair, Rudy and his family bravely decided to have both of his legs amputated. He learned to use prosthetic legs to get around.

With his prosthetic legs, there was no limit to Rudy's energy. At six, he tried swimming and loved it. He was fast, too! He joined a local swim team with the goal of winning a gold medal at the 2004 Paralympics.

At eight years old, Rudy was running and competing in relay triathlons. He completed his first solo triathlon when he was just 10 years old, and decided that his next goal would be to complete an Ironman triathlon.

Rudy trained hard, continuing to practice his skills in all of the sports he loved. In the 2004 Paralympics, 16-year-old Rudy made his dreams come true. Not only did he win the gold medal he wanted, but he also broke the world record in his class.

Since then, he continues to break records, win medals, and achieve his dreams. He completed his first Ironman, and now he has a new goal: to finish in less time. But he knows practice and training will be the key.

"It will come," says Rudy. "I just need to be patient. It's a very grueling training cycle. It's a 90-percent mental thing and a 10-percent physical thing."

Now, Rudy is a spokesperson for the Challenged Athletes Foundation, which helps young challenged athletes with their goals. Rudy makes it seem as though the impossible is possible. He has inspired young athletes all over the world to work hard to make their goals a reality.

Name: _____   **Date:** _____

PRACTICE MAKES PROGRESS

Directions: Some people say that "practice makes perfect," but what if instead we said that "practice makes progress"? Because even if the result isn't perfect, when you practice, you always make progress.

Rudy Garcia-Tolson was determined to achieve his goals. To make his dreams come true, he practiced and trained relentlessly. Think about Rudy's story as you answer the questions below. Then share your answers with a partner.

1. What are three words you would use to describe Rudy? How are you like Rudy?

   _____

   _____

   _____

2. Name one of Rudy's goals. Did he achieve it? If so, what do you think it took to accomplish it?

   _____

   _____

   _____

3. Rudy has said, "A brave heart is a powerful weapon." How do you think being brave has helped Rudy achieve his dreams?

   _____

   _____

   _____

4. Rudy doesn't seem to let anything get in his way. His positive attitude helps him tackle any challenge. How do you think having a positive, "can-do" attitude helps you?

   _____

   _____

   _____

5. What is one thing you will take away from reading Rudy's story?

   _____

   _____

Name: _____ **Date:** _____

· · · · · · · · · WALK A MILE · · · · · · · ·

It's said that you can't really understand someone else's life until you walk a mile in their shoes.

Directions: Watch the video *A Day in the Life: Rudy Garcia-Tolson* to get a sense of what it is like to be Rudy. Then form a small group with three to four other students. Choose one of the questions below, and discuss how you think Rudy would respond. Write your answer on the lines, and then share your group's answer with the class.

(1) You are told your practice time isn't fast enough to qualify for the race. What will you do?

(2) Another student says you will never be good enough to compete on the team. What do you say?

(3) A teacher lets you know that unless you score 90% or higher on the next test, you may not get a passing grade for the class. How do you prepare?

> Question chosen: #_____

_____

_____

_____

_____

_____

_____

_____

_____

_____

_____

_____

_____

_____

_____

Name: _____   **Date:** _____

· · · · · · · · · · A REAL JUGGLING ACT · · · · · · · ·

As you have learned, practice makes progress, not perfection! In this activity, you are going to learn a new skill and practice it. You will record your progress below, and then cheer on your fellow classmates to help encourage their practice, too.

Record the time it takes you to get it the first time. Then record the time it takes to make it five times in a row.

Follow these directions:

1. Stand on one leg and lift the other leg so your thigh is parallel to the floor (about a 90-degree angle).

2. Hold the tennis ball in your hand on the same side as your lifted leg.

3. Toss the ball over your lifted leg, and move the same hand under that leg to catch it.

After you become an expert on one side, switch to the other. Once you have mastered the catch, see if you can keep your lifted leg still. Then try to increase your speed! Record your best time in the "My record" star.

Left side, 1st time:

Left side, 5 times:

Right side, 1st time:

My record:

Right side, 5 times:

Name: _____   Date: _____

· · · · · · · · · · · CHANGE THE WORLD · · · · · · · · · · ·

"First they said I couldn't walk. Then they said I would never run. Competing at the Paralympics? Don't even try. They told me that double amputees should stay in a chair. Look how that turned out. Everyone says you cannot change the world—just the people around you. The people around me say that I've changed their life. I guess now it's time to change the world."—Rudy Garcia-Tolson

Once you start practicing and improving, you can achieve anything you want. Just like Rudy, you could change the world.

What is something you would like to practice and improve? How do you want to change the world?

_____

_____

_____

_____

_____

_____

_____

_____

_____

_____

_____

_____

_____

_____

_____

_____

_____

_____

★I★value THOUGHTFUL FEEDBACK.

> "It matters not what someone is born, but what they grow to be."
>
> J.K. Rowling

The ability to give and receive feedback is a critical piece in a student's growth mindset. It's important for students to learn that feedback doesn't equal failure, and that there is always an opportunity to adapt and grow.

★ Reading Passage: J.K. Rowling

One of the most successful authors in history faced numerous rejections, but it was feedback from a young reader that opened the door to her success.

★ Short-Answer Activity: Fantastic Feedback

Students will learn the definition of feedback, and reflect on lessons learned from the reading passage and their own experiences.

★ Small-Group Activity: Share Your Story

Working with a partner, students will role-play to pitch a creative story to each other. They will each have an opportunity to give and receive feedback.

★ Whole-Class Activity: Just Like Magic

Building on the small-group activity, students will develop the first chapter of a creative story and present it to the class. You may opt to make this a timed writing assignment or place a word-count limit to provide time for all students to share what they create with the class for feedback. Before feedback is given, discuss the included feedback rules as a class.

★ Journal Prompt: Feedback, Not Failure

Students will reflect on the experience of giving and receiving feedback, to discover how it was helpful for them and how they will use feedback in the future.

★ Growing Beyond

Establish feedback partnerships in the class. Fostering trusting relationship pairs will help students feel comfortable sharing feedback with one another. Post the rules of feedback in the class so that students have a visual reminder to be kind, specific, and helpful with their feedback.

Name: _____   Date: _____

J.K. ROWLING

J.K. Rowling, famous author of the *Harry Potter* books, was once just a struggling writer.

As a young girl, Joanne Rowling always knew she wanted to be a writer. She loved books, and she wrote her first story when she was just six years old. When she was 11, she wrote her first novel about seven cursed diamonds.

Many years later, she was a young, single mom waiting for a train that was late. As she waited, a story idea formed in her mind. The world of *Harry Potter* was born.

For five years, she took many notes and mapped out a series of seven books. Most of her notes were just scribbles on scraps of paper. She took her notes with her everywhere and wrote more whenever she could.

Chapter by chapter, *Harry Potter* came to life. When the first book was complete, she sent it out to publishers to see if anyone would take it.

But all she received back was disappointment. Twelve different publishers rejected her story, many without a reason. Joanne refused to give up though, and eventually, someone wanted her book.

That person was an eight-year-old girl named Alice. Because of the feedback Alice gave her father, who happened to be the chairman of Bloomsbury Children's Books, *Harry Potter* got published.

After reading the first chapter her dad gave her, Alice demanded the rest of the book. So, Joanne got her book deal, although she was asked to change her pen name to "J.K. Rowling."

Not everyone thought it would be a bestseller, though. Joanne's editor told her to "get a day job" in case the book wasn't a hit.

Of course, she proved them all wrong, and the *Harry Potter* books were a tremendous success. Joanne, or J.K., is one of the most successful authors in history—thanks to the feedback of eight-year-old Alice.

Name: _____   **Date:** _____

FANTASTIC FEEDBACK

⭐ What is feedback?

When you give feedback to someone, you are telling them what you think. You may be giving a suggestion or piece of advice for how they can improve their work.

⭐ Why do we give feedback?

Feedback helps us to improve. Sometimes, others see something in our work that we missed, or they have an idea that will make it even better.

Directions: Considering J.K. Rowling's story, and your own experiences, write your answers to the questions below.

1. How do you think J.K. Rowling felt when so many different publishers rejected her draft of *Harry Potter*? Why do you think she kept submitting it to other publishers?

   _____

   _____

   _____

2. When was the last time you received feedback? Do you think it helped you improve? Why or why not?

   _____

   _____

   _____

3. Have you ever given feedback to someone else? How did they react when they received it?

   _____

   _____

   _____

4. What does it feel like when you receive feedback? Are you open to it, or do you get defensive? Why do you think you react this way?

   _____

   _____

   _____

Name: _____   **Date:** _____

· · · · · · · · · · SHARE YOUR STORY · · · · · · · · · ·

Directions: On your own, come up with a title and short summary for a new book. It can be a story about anything you want! It could be the next book in the *Harry Potter* series, another book series you enjoy, or something totally new and different.

Write your title and the summary of your story below. Then pair up with another student. One of you will be the "writer," and one of you will be the "editor."

Writer: Imagine you are pitching your story idea to your partner. Share the title and summary of your book. Be open to hearing feedback. Write down something helpful that you learned.

Editor: Listen carefully to your partner. Offer some suggestions or advice that might improve their pitch.

When you're done, switch places so that each of you has a chance to give and receive feedback.

My book title: _____

What my story is about:

Helpful feedback I received:

Name: _____ **Date:** _____

JUST LIKE MAGIC

Constructive feedback can help transform and improve your work—just like magic!

Directions: Building on the last activity, now you will write the first chapter of your book. When you're done, you will share it with your fellow students.

On a separate piece of paper, write the first chapter of your story. When it's your turn to share, you will need to listen carefully as you are receiving feedback about your work. Then you will need to listen to others tell their stories, so you can give them feedback, too.

When you are receiving feedback, remember to:

- ⭐ Listen, not argue.
- ⭐ Think about the feedback you've received.
- ⭐ Thank the person for their feedback.
- ⭐ Decide on your own if you would like to make any changes to your story based on the feedback you received.

When you are giving feedback, remember to:

- ⭐ Be clear, kind, and helpful.
- ⭐ State something you liked first.
- ⭐ Ask a question or give advice.

Write down the most valuable piece of feedback you received here, and what you will change in your story as a result of it:

Name: _____ Date: _____

• • • • • • • • • FEEDBACK, NOT FAILURE • • • • • • • •

J.K. Rowling said, "We do not need magic to change the world, we carry all the power we need inside ourselves already: we have the power to imagine better."

Just because you receive feedback doesn't mean you have failed. Sometimes, like J.K. Rowling, you just have to keep an open mind to the feedback you receive and keep trying.

Now that you have had a chance to give and receive feedback, do you see how it can help improve your work? What is something you have learned about feedback that will help you in the future?

_____
_____
_____
_____
_____
_____
_____
_____
_____
_____
_____
_____
_____
_____
_____
_____
_____
_____

I am CAPABLE of learning NEW THINGS.

> "Lots of people...would say, '...it's the worst thing imaginable, to be an architect and to lose your sight. I can't imagine anything worse.' But I quickly came to realize that the creative process is an intellectual process. It's how you think, so I just needed new tools."
>
> **Chris Downey**

To learn something new is always a challenge. But when students understand the possibility and the "power of yet," they realize that no challenge is insurmountable.

★ Reading Passage: Chris Downey

When architect Chris Downey lost his sight, others doubted he could still do his job. But Chris found joy in relearning how to live his life without sight.

★ Short-Answer Activity: Light in the Dark

After reading Chris's story, students will work in pairs and as individuals to reflect on Chris's approach to learning and their own capacity to learn new skills.

★ Small-Group Activity: Discover the Power of Yet

Students will discover the power of adding "yet" to statements like "I can't do this." On their own, they will write three things they haven't learned yet and three things that could help them learn. Then in pairs, they will share what they've learned with each other and provide encouragement to their partners.

★ Whole-Class Activity: Believe in the Power of Yet

Continuing the work of the small-group activity, students will focus on one skill or task and fill out a graphic organizer that helps them make a learning plan. Create a bulletin board or poster for the class to add their own learning goals to, and provide opportunities for regular check-ins on these goals. When they are achieved or mastered, offer a celebration or reward.

★ Journal Prompt: Just Not Yet

Students will reflect on what it feels like to tackle new learning challenges, as well as how they stay motivated to keep going.

★ Growing Beyond

Watch the 10-minute TED Talk *Chris Downey: Design with the blind in mind*. Ask students to note what Chris says was the most surprising thing he learned since losing his sight (the difference between experiencing the same places with and without sight). Ask them to reflect on what it might be like to experience the places they know in their own homes, classroom, and neighborhoods, without sight. What might they learn to notice if they weren't relying on their sight? Discuss findings as a class.

Name: _____   Date: _____

CHRIS DOWNEY

Chris Downey is an architect. He designs spaces that people live and work in, such as buildings and homes.

And he does it all without being able to see. Chris Downey is blind. He lost his sight after he had to have a tumor surgically removed from his brain.

When he was still recovering from surgery, a social worker came to visit him in the hospital. She told him she could help him find a new job, thinking that he would no longer be able to be an architect if he was blind.

But Chris didn't see it that way—literally. He thought of his new way of life as an opportunity to learn new things, and he was willing to work hard.

Chris's son, Renzo, was just 10 years old when his dad lost his vision. Chris knew he wanted to be a good example for his son and show him that taking on challenges is a part of life. So, with Renzo in mind, Chris started to learn what it meant to live his life as a blind man.

He had to learn how to get around, how to use public transportation, and how to work in the kitchen safely. Chris recalls what it felt like the first time he had to cross a major intersection by himself. "I remember that day, stepping off the curb and it was like you would have thought I was stepping into raging waters. Take a deep breath and go for it. You gotta push through it."

Chris was back to work in a month. He found ways that he could still design spaces, even without his vision. He just needed some new tools to help him. Now, he creates his ideas by using wax sticks he can mold to show his plans. Chris also uses a special printer that embosses his drawings so that he can touch and feel them on paper.

Without sight, Chris now relies more on his other senses to help him. He listens for the sounds around him, and uses his senses of smell and touch to guide him.

Chris is still working as an architect. Now, he designs spaces for blind people. "I am absolutely convinced I'm a better architect today than I was sighted," he says.

Name: _____   Date: _____

· · · · · · · · · · · · LIGHT IN THE DARK · · · · · · · · · ·

Directions: Now that you have read Chris Downey's story, find a partner and talk about what you discovered. What is the one thing you will remember about Chris's story? Then, on your own, answer the questions below.

1. When Chris lost his sight, he had to learn how to do everything all over again. Can you think of three things that would be challenging to do if you couldn't see?

_____

_____

_____

_____

2. It might have been easier for Chris to give up on his career as an architect and try to find something else to do. What do you think made Chris determined to find new tools to help him do his job?

_____

_____

_____

_____

3. Chris talks about how scary it was to cross the street for the first time without sight. Can you think of a time when you learned something new and had to do it on your own for the first time? What was that like?

_____

_____

_____

_____

4. What is something new you would like to learn to do? Why do you want to learn this?

_____

_____

_____

_____

Name: _____   Date: _____

DISCOVER THE POWER OF YET

When something is hard or new, sometimes we say to ourselves, "I can't do that." But there is one word you can add to that sentence that changes everything: YET.

When you say, "I can't do that YET," you are allowing some space for you to learn how to do the thing you want to do.

Directions: Think of three things you haven't learned yet. Then list three things you could do to help you learn your "yet." When your list is complete, find a partner and share your lists. Talk about how you could support each other in learning your "yets."

I can't do this YET...

But if I do this, I will learn!

1. _____
2. _____
3. _____

I can't do this YET...

But if I do this, I will learn!

1. _____
2. _____
3. _____

I can't do this YET...

But if I do this, I will learn!

1. _____
2. _____
3. _____

Name: _____ **Date:** _____

BELIEVE IN THE POWER OF YET

Directions: Focus your attention on one of the three things you haven't learned yet. Fill out the graphic organizer below to help you make a plan for turning your "yet" into new learning!

What I will gain by learning this:

Who can help me learn this:

I can't do this YET...
but soon, I will learn!

How I will feel when I learn this:

What can help motivate me:

Name: _____   **Date:** _____

JUST NOT YET

Vincent Van Gogh said, "I am always doing what I cannot do yet, in order to learn how to do it."

Learning new things can be challenging, but if you approach new learning opportunities with a can-do attitude, anything is possible.

When is the last time you tried to learn something new? Describe it. Was it hard? How does it feel when you have to work a little harder to learn something? How do you stay motivated to keep learning?

_____

_____

_____

_____

_____

_____

_____

_____

_____

_____

_____

_____

_____

_____

_____

_____

_____

_____

_____

I can KEEP GOING when THINGS are TOUGH.

> "So often in life, things that you regard as an impediment turn out to be great, good fortune."
>
> Ruth Bader Ginsburg

As students face new challenges, they will need to learn perseverance and grit to keep going. In this unit, they will discover what it means to show grit and how it can help push them even further toward success.

★ Reading Passage: Ruth Bader Ginsburg

Despite the discrimination iconic Supreme Court Justice Ruth Bader Ginsburg faced throughout her career, her grittiness has helped her achieve what seemed impossible.

★ Short-Answer Activity: Grab Some GRIT

After reading Ruth Bader Ginsburg's story, students will reflect on what they learned and will be presented with a new definition of *GRIT*.

★ Small-Group Activity: Do You Have Grit?

Students will rate themselves on their current level of grit and provide evidence of a time when they have shown their own grittiness.

★ Whole-Class Activity: A Gritty Gathering

In this activity, students will have to work together and persevere to solve a problem. Lay a piece of rope in a large circle on the floor—big enough for all of the students to sit inside the circle. Invite them all to sit in the circle, and once they are there, praise them for working together. Now, make the circle smaller. Ask them to try again. Keep making the circle smaller, and encourage them to get creative with their solutions. They may also ask questions, such as "Does my whole body have to be in the circle?" Afterward, give them time to reflect on what they learned.

★ Journal Prompt: My Gritty Hero

Students will think of someone in their life who has demonstrated grit, and reflect on that person's heroic journey and how it has influenced them.

★ Growing Beyond

As a class, read *Notorious RBG: The Life and Times of Ruth Bader Ginsburg* (Young Readers' Edition) by Irin Carmon and Shana Knizhnik. Discuss one or more of the historical cases in which Justice Ginsburg has ruled, and ask students to argue for either the majority opinion or the dissenting opinion.

Name: _____   Date: _____

RUTH BADER GINSBURG

When Ruth Bader Ginsburg graduated from law school, she couldn't find a job. Even though she was an excellent student, there was one big reason no one wanted to hire her: she is a woman.

This wasn't the first time she had challenges she had to overcome. Ruth went to law school at Harvard, where she was one of only nine women in a class of 500 students.

Ruth's husband was also a lawyer and was offered a job in New York. So, Ruth transferred to Columbia Law School. She graduated first in her class.

But law firms were not interested in hiring her. They told her that they didn't want a woman working for them, especially not when she had a young daughter at home that needed caring for. Ruth was disappointed and upset, but she didn't give up.

Finally, one of Ruth's professors helped her find a job as a clerk for another judge. He convinced the judge that Ruth would be an excellent lawyer. The judge wasn't sure, but he agreed to give Ruth a chance.

Ruth Bader Ginsburg has always believed in gender equality, or in other words, that women and men are equal and deserve the same rights.

She is strongly in favor of equal rights for all, and her work for the American Civil Liberties Union had her arguing six cases in front of the Supreme Court.

In 1993, she was appointed to the US Supreme Court. She became only the second woman in American history to serve as a Supreme Court justice.

No matter what obstacles she has faced, or how tough it was to continue fighting for what she believes in, Ruth Bader Ginsburg has shown true grit. She has said, "Fight for the things that you care about. But do it in a way that will lead others to join you."

Even though she is not always able to sway the opinions of some of her colleagues in the Supreme Court, she has never given up hope. "Dissents speak to a future age," she says, because she hopes that even if they don't agree with her now, they will someday.

Name: _____   **Date:** _____

GRAB SOME GRIT

Ruth Bader Ginsburg had to fight through some tough times to accomplish all that she has. No matter the challenge, she never gave up, and she stayed focused on her goals.

You could call this GRIT. GRIT stands for:

- ⭐ **G**ive it your all.
- ⭐ **R**edo if necessary.
- ⭐ **I**gnore giving up.
- ⭐ **T**ake time to do it right.

People with GRIT never give up, even when things get tough.

Directions: Thinking about Ruth Bader Ginsburg's story, write your answers to the questions below.

1. How do you think Ruth Bader Ginsburg felt when she kept getting turned down for jobs, simply because she is a woman?

   _____

   _____

2. Ruth has said, "Women belong in all places where decisions are being made." At one time, many people did not agree with her. How do you think it felt for Ruth to stick to her beliefs, even when everyone around her disagreed?

   _____

   _____

3. Do you think that Ruth Bader Ginsburg has GRIT? Why or why not? Use the passage to support your opinion.

   _____

   _____

   _____

4. Do you know someone who has GRIT? What qualities does this person have that makes you think of them as gritty? How have they demonstrated GRIT?

   _____

   _____

   _____

Name: _____   Date: _____

DO YOU HAVE GRIT?

Directions: How gritty are you? Take this short quiz to find out. On your own, read each statement and mark the column that reflects how often you feel this way.

	Always True	Sometimes True	Rarely True
1. I have a long-term goal for my future.	☐	☐	☐
2. I don't quit when things get hard.	☐	☐	☐
3. I always finish what I start.	☐	☐	☐
4. I think mistakes are just ways to help me learn.	☐	☐	☐
5. I look for ways to improve.	☐	☐	☐
6. I give my best effort.	☐	☐	☐

If most of your answers are "Always True" or "Sometimes True," you already have grit! If most of your answers are "Rarely True," then grit is something you are still learning.

Directions: We are all gritty sometimes. Can you think of a time when you showed grit? Give evidence of your grittiness, and write your grit story here. When you're done, find a partner and share your answers with each other.

I showed grit when...

Name: _____   **Date:** _____

A GRITTY GATHERING

Here is another way we can define *grit*.

- ⭐ **G** is for Goals.
- ⭐ **R** is for Resilience.
- ⭐ **I** is for Intention.
- ⭐ **T** is for Time.

People who are gritty pursue a long-term, intentional goal over time. And when things get tough, they bounce back and keep going—they are resilient.

Directions: In this class activity, you will pursue a single goal. It's going to get tougher as you go, but if you show some grit and work together creatively, you will achieve the goal!

Listen for directions from your teacher. When the activity is complete, come back and record what you learned.

What I learned about grit

Name: _____ **Date:** _____

· · · · · · · · · · · MY GRITTY HERO · · · · · · · · · · ·

Remembering the definition of *grit*, think of someone you would consider a gritty hero. It could be someone in your family, a friend, or someone famous you look up to.

★ What was the goal your hero had?

★ What resilience did your hero show?

★ What was your hero's intention?

★ How much time did it take your hero to achieve their goal?

Finally, write about something you have personally learned from your gritty hero.

_____

_____

_____

_____

_____

_____

_____

_____

_____

_____

_____

_____

_____

_____

_____

_____

_____

_____

I can TRAIN MY BRAIN.

> "Do the best you can until you know better. Then when you know better, do better."
>
> Maya Angelou

The discovery that our brains can be trained can be a revelation that empowers students to learn beyond their wildest dreams.

⭐ Reading Passage: Maya Angelou

Award-winning author, poet, and civil-rights activist Maya Angelou is known for her strong voice. But she lost it for a time, when she stopped speaking for five years as a child. How she learned to find her voice again is a beautiful example of training the brain to learn something new.

⭐ Short-Answer Activity: Train Your Brain

Students will discover that the brain is an ever-changing, ever-growing "muscle" that gets stronger with exercise. As they reflect on Maya Angelou's story, they will uncover why it's important to train your brain. After answering questions, they will form a group and share their responses.

⭐ Small-Group Activity: Fixed vs. Growth Mindset

Discuss with students the definitions of fixed and growth mindsets. Then have them pair up to complete this activity in which they will place mindset statements in their correct places.

⭐ Whole-Class Activity: Born to Learn

As a class, watch the short video "You Can Learn Anything" from Khan Academy, which introduces the idea that we, as humans, are born to learn. Then ask students to reflect on what it means to be "born to learn." Afterward, ask students to complete the fill-in-the-blank letter: a letter their older self is writing to their younger self, with advice on learning.

⭐ Journal Prompt: New Attitude

Just as important as the ability to learn is the willingness to learn. Responding to the questions, students will examine their own attitudes toward learning.

⭐ Growing Beyond

Read some of Maya Angelou's poetry or prose to the class. Have each student read a portion aloud to help find their voice, just as Maya did. Ask them to write their own poems and speak them aloud to the class.

Name: _____ Date: _____

MAYA ANGELOU

Maya Angelou was an award-winning author, an actor, and a poet. She is known for speaking out and using her voice. But when she was a child, she stopped speaking for five years.

After she was hurt by her mother's boyfriend, Maya testified against him in court. The man was set free but died soon after. Believing her words had harmed him, eight-year-old Maya was scared.

"I thought, my voice [hurt] him," she said. "I [hurt] that man because I told his name. And then I thought I would never speak again, because my voice would [hurt] anyone."

The power of her own words terrified her. So she stopped speaking altogether, except to her brother, Bailey.

In her silent world, Maya turned to books for comfort. She loved to read, especially poetry.

She also learned to listen more carefully, especially to her teacher, Mrs. Flowers. Mrs. Flowers encouraged Maya's reading, but she told her that she couldn't truly appreciate poetry without speaking it aloud.

Mrs. Flowers told her, "Words mean more than what is set down on paper. It takes the human voice to infuse them with the shades of deeper meaning."

At first, Maya resisted this idea and kept silent. But finally, when she was 13, she tried reading a poem aloud and felt it come alive. Slowly, she began speaking again. But she took what she had learned during those silent years with her.

Maya went on to accomplish so much in her life—as a poet, an author, and a speaker. She became an instructor, too, teaching poetry at Wake Forest University. She said, "I found after teaching one year that I had misunderstood my calling. I had thought that I was a writer who could teach. I found to my surprise that I was actually a teacher who could write."

Maya wrote the story of her life in her autobiography, *I Know Why the Caged Bird Sings*. The book became the first nonfiction bestseller written by an African-American woman.

Name: _____   Date: _____

TRAIN YOUR BRAIN

Our brains are always growing and changing, which means we can always learn something new!

Directions: On your own, answer these questions. Then form a group with two other students and share your answers with one another.

1. When Maya stopped speaking, she started reading more, and she trained herself to listen more carefully to what was going on around her. What is something you have trained your brain to do?

   _____

   _____

   _____

   _____

2. Did you know your brain is like a muscle? The more you use it, the stronger it grows! Working on brainteasers or word or number games boosts your brain activity, improves your memory, and helps your brain process information faster. How have you challenged your brain lately?

   _____

   _____

   _____

3. Your brain runs on electricity. It produces enough power to light up a 25-watt light bulb! Maybe that's why they call it "sparking" your imagination. Poetry is what sparked Maya's imagination and made her want to speak again. What is something that helps spark your imagination?

   _____

   _____

   _____

4. When Maya found her voice again, she began speaking and writing her own poetry and stories. What do you think she learned during the time that she was silent?

   _____

   _____

   _____

   _____

Name: _____   **Date:** _____

FIXED VS. GROWTH MINDSET

Having a *fixed mindset* means you think if you're not good at something, you should just give up. Having a *growth mindset* means you think that with effort and perseverance, you can learn and do anything you want to.

Directions: Where do the statements below fit? Pair up with another student. Cut out the statements at the bottom and place them where they belong—either as part of a fixed mindset or a growth mindset.

Fixed Mindset

Growth Mindset

★ I can't do this.	★ I'm not good at this.	★ I can always improve.
★ This is too hard.	★ I can learn from my mistakes.	★ I will keep trying.
★ I will try to figure it out.	★ I will do my best.	★ I'll never get this right.
★ I don't know yet.	★ It's good enough.	★ I want to learn.

Name: _____ **Date:** _____

BORN TO LEARN

What does it mean that you are born to learn? Maybe it means that we all start somewhere. Maya Angelou said, "I've learned that I still have a lot to learn."

Directions: Knowing that you are born to learn, write a letter to yourself from the future.

Imagine that you are 75 years old, and you want to write a letter to yourself at the age you are now. Give some advice about what you have learned. Use the prompts below to guide you as you write your letter.

Dear _____ ,
(your name)
   This is what I want to tell you about learning:

   I never thought you could train yourself to _____ ,
but you did it! Here's how:

   If there's one thing I could say to inspire you, it would be this:

   And one last thing... Don't forget to do this:

                              Yours,

                              _____
                              (your name)

Name: _____ **Date:** _____

NEW ATTITUDE

Maya Angelou once said, "If you don't like something, change it. If you can't change it, change your attitude."

You have to be willing to learn. What is your attitude about learning new things? Do you approach learning with a positive attitude or a negative attitude? What have you discovered about having a growth mindset that may help you learn in the future?

_____

_____

_____

_____

_____

_____

_____

_____

_____

_____

_____

_____

_____

_____

_____

_____

_____

_____

_____

_____

_____

MEETING STANDARDS

Most of the activities in *Change Your Mindset: Growth Mindset Activities for the Classroom* meet one or more of the following Common Core State Standards © Copyright 2010. National Governors Association Center for Best Practices and Council of Chief State School Officers. All rights reserved. For more information about the Common Core State Standards, go to *http://www.corestandards.org/* or *http://www.teachercreated.com/standards/*.

Grade 5	
Reading: Informational Text	**Activity Title (Unit #)**
Range of Reading and Level of Text Complexity	
ELA.RI.5.10: By the end of the year, read and comprehend informational texts, including history/social studies, science, and technical texts, at the high end of the grades 4–5 text complexity band independently and proficiently.	Katharine Hepburn (1), Wilma Rudolph (2), Bruno Mars (3), Jessica Cox (4), Lin-Manuel Miranda (5), Cesar Chavez (6), Malala Yousafzai (7), Rudy Garcia-Tolson (8), J.K. Rowling (9), Chris Downey (10), Ruth Bader Ginsburg (11), Growing Beyond (11), Maya Angelou (12)
Writing	**Activity Title (Unit #)**
Text Types and Purposes	
ELA.W.5.2: Write informative/explanatory texts to examine a topic and convey ideas and information clearly.	Growing Beyond (7), My Gritty Hero (11)
ELA.W.5.3: Write narratives to develop real or imagined experiences or events using effective technique, descriptive details, and clear event sequences.	The Greatest Day (5), Share Your Story (9), Just Not Yet (10), Do You Have Grit? (11)
Production and Distribution of Writing	
ELA.W.5.4: Produce clear and coherent writing in which the development and organization are appropriate to task, purpose, and audience.	Best of the Best (1), Common Ground (1), Be Your Best (1), Determined to Succeed (2), Toss Up (2), Best Effort (2), Master Plan (2), Making Mistakes (3), The Book of Mistakes (3), Mistakes or Lessons? (3), Learning to Fly (4), Fearlessly Brave (4), 3-2-1 Go! (5), Get SMART (5), A Vision for the Future (5), The Greatest Day (5), Staying Strong (6), Acts of Courage (6), Have Some Courage (6), Face the Fear (6), Find Another Path (7), App-tastic Solutions (7), Overcoming Hurdles (7), Growing Beyond (7), Practice Makes Progress (8), Walk a Mile (8), Change the World (8), Fantastic Feedback (9), Share Your Story (9), Just Like Magic (9), Feedback, Not Failure (9), Light in the Dark (10), Discover the Power of Yet (10), Believe in the Power of Yet (10), Just Not Yet (10), Grab Some GRIT (11), Do You Have Grit? (11), A Gritty Gathering (11), My Gritty Hero (11), Train Your Brain (12), Born to Learn (12), New Attitude (12), Growing Beyond (12)
Speaking & Listening	**Activity Title (Unit #)**
Comprehension and Collaboration	
ELA.SL.5.1: Engage effectively in a range of collaborative discussions (one-on-one, in groups, and teacher-led) with diverse partners on *grade 5 topics and texts*, building on others' ideas and expressing their own clearly.	Best of the Best (1), Common Ground (1), Growing Beyond (1), Best Effort (2), Growing Beyond (2), Making Mistakes (3), The Book of Mistakes (3), Learning to Fly (4), Get SMART (5), A Vision for the Future (5), Staying Strong (6), Acts of Courage (6), Growing Beyond (6), Find Another Path (7), 30 Ways (7), App-tastic Solutions (7), Practice Makes Progress (8), Walk a Mile (8), Share Your Story (9), Just Like Magic (9), Light in the Dark (10), Discover the Power of Yet (10), Growing Beyond (10), Do You Have Grit? (11), Growing Beyond (11), Train Your Brain (12)
Presentation of Knowledge and Ideas	
ELA.SL.5.4: Report on a topic or text or present an opinion, sequencing ideas logically and using appropriate facts and relevant, descriptive details to support main ideas or themes; speak clearly at an understandable pace.	App-tastic Solutions (7), Walk a Mile (8), Share Your Story (9), Just Like Magic (9), Growing Beyond (11), Growing Beyond (12)

Grade 6	
Reading: Informational Text	**Activity Title (Unit #)**
Range of Reading and Level of Text Complexity	
ELA.RI.6.10: By the end of the year, read and comprehend literary nonfiction in the grades 6–8 text complexity band proficiently, with scaffolding as needed at the high end of the range.	Katharine Hepburn (1), Wilma Rudolph (2), Bruno Mars (3), Jessica Cox (4), Lin-Manuel Miranda (5), Cesar Chavez (6), Malala Yousafzai (7), Rudy Garcia-Tolson (8), J.K. Rowling (9), Chris Downey (10), Ruth Bader Ginsburg (11), Growing Beyond (11), Maya Angelou (12)
Writing	**Activity Title (Unit #)**
Text Types and Purposes	
ELA.W.6.2: Write informative/explanatory texts to examine a topic and convey ideas, concepts, and information through the selection, organization, and analysis of relevant content.	Growing Beyond (7), My Gritty Hero (11)
ELA.W.6.3: Write narratives to develop real or imagined experiences or events using effective technique, relevant descriptive details, and well-structured event sequences.	The Greatest Day (5), Share Your Story (9), Just Not Yet (10), Do You Have Grit? (11)
Production and Distribution of Writing	
ELA.W.6.4: Produce clear and coherent writing in which the development, organization, and style are appropriate to task, purpose, and audience.	Best of the Best (1), Common Ground (1), Be Your Best (1), Determined to Succeed (2), Toss Up (2), Best Effort (2), Master Plan (2), Making Mistakes (3), The Book of Mistakes (3), Mistakes or Lessons? (3), Learning to Fly (4), Fearlessly Brave (4), 3-2-1 Go! (5), Get SMART (5), A Vision for the Future (5), The Greatest Day (5), Staying Strong (6), Acts of Courage (6), Have Some Courage (6), Face the Fear (6), Find Another Path (7), App-tastic Solutions (7), Overcoming Hurdles (7), Growing Beyond (7), Practice Makes Progress (8), Walk a Mile (8), Change the World (8), Fantastic Feedback (9), Share Your Story (9), Just Like Magic (9), Feedback, Not Failure (9), Light in the Dark (10), Discover the Power of Yet (10), Believe in the Power of Yet (10), Just Not Yet (10), Grab Some GRIT (11), Do You Have Grit? (11), A Gritty Gathering (11), My Gritty Hero (11), Train Your Brain (12), Born to Learn (12), New Attitude (12), Growing Beyond (12)
Speaking & Listening	**Activity Title (Unit #)**
Comprehension and Collaboration	
ELA.SL.6.1: Engage effectively in a range of collaborative discussions (one-on-one, in groups, and teacher-led) with diverse partners on *grade 6 topics, texts, and issues*, building on others' ideas and expressing their own clearly.	Best of the Best (1), Common Ground (1), Growing Beyond (1), Best Effort (2), Growing Beyond (2), Making Mistakes (3), The Book of Mistakes (3), Learning to Fly (4), Get SMART (5), A Vision for the Future (5), Staying Strong (6), Acts of Courage (6), Growing Beyond (6), Find Another Path (7), 30 Ways (7), App-tastic Solutions (7), Practice Makes Progress (8), Walk a Mile (8), Share Your Story (9), Just Like Magic (9), Light in the Dark (10), Discover the Power of Yet (10), Growing Beyond (10), Do You Have Grit? (11), Growing Beyond (11), Train Your Brain (12)
Presentation of Knowledge and Ideas	
ELA.SL.6.4: Present claims and findings, sequencing ideas logically and using pertinent descriptions, facts, and details to accentuate main ideas or themes; use appropriate eye contact, adequate volume, and clear pronunciation.	App-tastic Solutions (7), Walk a Mile (8), Share Your Story (9), Just Like Magic (9), Growing Beyond (11), Growing Beyond (12)